DiG iT:
HiSTORY FROM
OBJECTS

The Vikings

John Malam

PowerKiDS press.

New York

Published in 2011 by The Rosen Publishing Group Inc.
29 East 21st Street, New York, NY 10010

First Edition

Produced for Wayland by Calcium
Design: Paul Myerscough
Editor: Sarah Eason
Editor for Wayland: Camilla Lloyd
Illustrations: Geoff Ward
Picture Research: Maria Joannou
Consultant: John Malam

Library of Congress Cataloging-in-Publication Data

Malam, John, 1957-
The Vikings / by John Malam. — 1st ed.
    p. cm. — (Dig it: history from objects)
ISBN 978-1-4488-3286-6 (library binding)
1. Vikings—Juvenile literature. 2. Viking antiquities—Juvenile literature. I. Title.
DL66.M35 2011
948'.022—dc22

                    2010023867

Photographs:
Alamy Images: Interfoto 25t, Interfoto/Fine Arts 17b; Corbis: The Art Archive 13b,
Ted Spiegel 13t, Werner Forman 17t, 23b; Getty Images: Dorling Kindersley/Liz
McAulay 12; Rex Features: Richard Gardner 18, Nils Jorgensen 8; Shutterstock:
Algol 14t, Andrew Barker 5, 16, 26t, Bluecrayola 11t, 27b, JackF 11b, 26c, Roman
Kaplanski 3, 14b, Andrei Nekrassov 22, 26b, Tyler Olson 20, Photo25th 7, 27t, Igor
Plotnikov 6, Anna Stasevska 23t, Dusan Zidar 19; Topham Picturepoint: Firth 10;
Wayland Picture Library: 21b, 24; Wikimedia Commons: 15, Andrew Dunn 25b,
Hedning 4, 21t, Thomas Ormston 9. Cover photograph: Shutterstock/Photo25th

Manufactured in China
CPSIA Compliance Information: Batch #WAW1102PK: For Further Information
contact Rosen Publishing, New York, New York at 1-800-237-9932

Contents

Who Were the Vikings?

The Vikings came from Scandinavia. This is an area in northeast Europe where Norway, Sweden, and Denmark are today. The Vikings **conquered** and **settled** new lands for about 300 years, from 800 CE to 1100 CE. This is called the Viking Age.

The Viking World

The Vikings were great travelers. They explored Europe, North Africa, the Middle East, and the islands of the north Atlantic Ocean. Shetland, the Faroe Islands, Iceland, and Greenland were stepping stones for their journeys, taking them farther west. Eventually, they crossed the Atlantic and reached Canada, becoming the first Europeans to set foot on the North American continent.

 *Norway and Sweden have mountains, forests, and **fjords** (say fee-ords). Denmark does not have any mountains and is flat.*

SEA RAIDERS

The word Viking may come from the Scandinavian word "viking," meaning pirate or sea raider.

Traders and Raiders

On their travels, the Vikings came into contact with many different people. They were known as violent **warriors** but also as **traders**. As traders, Vikings sailed along rivers and across seas. They took jewels, walrus **ivory**, furs, and **slaves**, which they traded for silver, gold, silk, spice, honey, and wine. They raided **monasteries** and towns, stealing objects and taking prisoners.

Settlers

Many Vikings moved away from their homeland. There was a shortage of farmland in Scandinavia, so they searched for new places to live. About 10,000 Vikings settled in Iceland, and 3,000 went to live in Greenland. Ireland, Britain, Russia, and France also became their homes. Wherever they settled, they took the Viking way of life with them.

Key
Viking homelands

Norway, Sweden, and Denmark were the homelands of the Vikings.

What Does it Tell Us?

Ships or boats were extremely important to Vikings. Longships carried warriors on raiding missions across Europe. Huge trading ships moved people, animals, and **goods** over great distances.

7

Towns and Homes

There were no real towns in Scandinavia before the age of the Vikings. Instead, the landscape was dotted with farms and a few marketplaces. During the time of the Vikings, the first towns appeared.

Trading Goods

There were some marketplaces in Scandinavia. In these places, such as in Helgö in Sweden, large numbers of people gathered to trade goods. Marketplaces were used at certain times of the year. For a few days, traders and craftspeople sold goods from **stalls** in the open air.

First Towns

At Ribe in Denmark, people stayed at the market all year round. By the early 800s CE, it had become the first town in Scandinavia. Towns also developed in places where the Vikings settled, such as Dublin (Ireland), Novgorod (Russia), and York (England).

Town streets were busy, narrow places where garbage was often left lying around.

What Does it Tell Us?

This longhouse, at Stöng, Iceland, is a copy of a Viking longhouse. It has been made using the same materials the Vikings used. It shows us that the Vikings covered their roofs in thick turf to keep the house warm.

Longhouses

In the countryside, Vikings lived in longhouses. They were farmhouses that looked like barns or halls. The family lived at one end and their farm animals at the other. In the middle was an open fire used for cooking and for keeping the house warm.

Townhouses

Townhouses were smaller than longhouses. Most were single-story buildings, usually made from wood, **wattle and daub**, and **turf**. Some parts were used as workshops where craftsmen could make their goods.

SMALL TOWN

All Viking towns were small compared to towns today. Even Hedeby, in Denmark, which was one of the largest towns, had fewer than 2,000 people.

Farming and Food

Most Vikings were farmers. They cleared forests or used rough land to make farms. On small farms the work was done by the farmer and his family. On larger farms, the Vikings used **slaves** to do the work.

Crops

Cabbages, onions, beans, and peas were the main vegetables grown. The main crops were grains, especially oats, barley, and rye. Oats were used to make oatmeal. Barley and rye were made into a **yeast**-free bread. It was too cold to grow wheat in many Viking lands, so wheat was brought in by traders.

Food and Drinks

Meat came from pigs, sheep, goats, and geese, and also from deer, horses, seals, and whales. It was roasted, boiled, stewed, or made into sausages, then served with vegetables. Vikings near the sea ate fish, shellfish, and seabirds and their eggs. Butter and cheese came from milk, and honey was used to sweeten food. They drank milk, barley beer, and an alcoholic drink called **mead**, made from honey.

Food was cooked over open fires inside houses.

FLAT BREAD

Viking bread was made without yeast, which meant it stayed flat and did not rise.

10

Mealtimes

Vikings had two meals a day—the "day meal," in the early morning, and the "night meal," in the early evening. Food was cooked over the house fire, and was served in wooden bowls and on wooden plates called platters. They used metal knives and wooden or horn spoons, but did not have forks. Cups were made from wood, except in rich households, where glass and silver ones were used.

 The Vikings cooked their food in pots such as these, above.

What Does it Tell Us?

Drinking horns like this were filled with beer or mead. They tell us that the Vikings enjoyed drinking. The horn could not be put down without spilling the contents— it had to be emptied all at once!

Clothes and Crafts

Viking women made clothes for their families. The poorer Vikings and slaves wore hard-wearing, practical clothes that were not fashionable. The clothes of richer Vikings were made from more expensive materials.

Viking Clothes

Women wore ankle-length dresses, over which were **tunics** held in place by shoulder brooches. Scarves and caps covered their heads. Men wore knee-length tunics and pants, and leather or wool caps. Both men and women wore flat leather shoes or boots and woolen socks. In cold weather, they wrapped up in warm cloaks of wool or fur. Children dressed as their parents did, but girls kept their heads uncovered, except in very cold weather.

Clothes for the Rich

Rich Vikings had clothes made from expensive silk from China. Traders bought them at markets in the east. The wealthy also had gold and silver threads woven into patterns on their clothes.

BAGGY PANTS

Vikings who met Arabs on their travels copied their clothes, and returned to Scandinavia wearing loose-fitting, baggy pants.

A Viking warrior would have worn a warm woolen tunic, pants, and tough, leather boots.

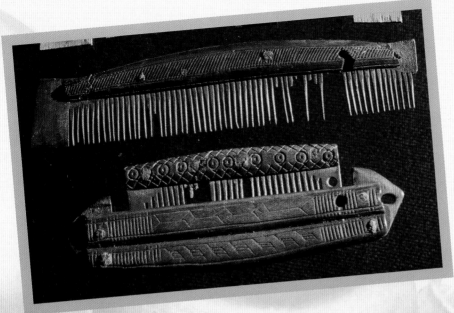

The teeth of Viking combs were close together to comb out knots and to catch head lice.

Viking Crafts

The Vikings were skilled at many crafts, and they produced a wide variety of everyday items. Pieces of animal bone and horn were made into combs, pins, and spoons. Woodworkers made cups, bowls, platters, barrels for ale, and furniture. Jewellers worked with **amber**, **jet**, and glass to make beads and necklaces. They also made brooches, clasps, and bracelets from **bronze** and silver.

What Does it Tell Us?

Brooches were always made of bronze metal. Rich women could have highly decorated brooches, which might also have been covered in a layer of gold.

13

Ships and Travel

The Vikings were great ship builders and travelers. They journeyed along rivers and sailed across wide seas. Several Viking ships have been found, which is how we know about them.

Trade and Ships

Viking ships were made from planks of wood, held together firmly with metal pins called rivets. A trader's ship was called a knarr. It was deep and wide with a big, square sail. Its main job was to carry goods—although knarrs also carried people. Knarrs took settlers to new homes, and it was probably knarrs that were the first ships to sail from Europe to North America.

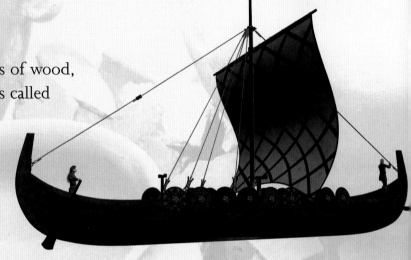

 A model of a Viking longship. These ships were used to transport bands of warriors.

Warships for Warriors

Viking warriors used longships. They are also known as dragonships, because a carving of a dragon was sometimes put at the prow (front). They had a sail, but most of the time they were rowed by the men on board. Longships were narrow and not too deep, so they could sail in shallow water and even come up onto beaches.

 The prow of a Viking longship, carved as a dragon.

What Does it Tell Us?

Sometimes important people were buried in ships. Two women's bodies were found in this ship. It was discovered at Oseberg in Norway and had been buried around 800 CE.

Crossing the Seas

Viking sailors were also explorers. The Viking Leif Ericsson was a great explorer. In around 1000 CE, he sailed west from Greenland in search of new land. After a few days, he came to a land of rocks and **glaciers**. He then sailed south along the coast to a place with woods, rivers, and wild grapes. He called it Vinland, which means Wine Land. We now know that he had reached the coast of Canada.

HEAVY LOAD

A knarr found at Hedeby, in Denmark, could carry a load weighing up to 38 tons—about the weight of six African elephants.

Warriors and Raiders

In 793 CE, Vikings from Norway attacked Lindisfarne Island, off the northeast coast of England. It was the first Viking raid in history, and marked the start of raids across western Europe.

Viking Raids

Towns, villages, and monasteries in Britain, Ireland, and France were attacked by Vikings. They were searching for gold, silver, and other valuable things. Gold and silver objects were cut into small pieces that could be easily carried and traded for goods, or melted down and made into new items. Prisoners were also taken and held for **ransom**. For example, the **abbot** of a French monastery was taken prisoner. He was only released after the French paid the Vikings an enormous amount of gold and silver.

Lindisfarne Island (also known as Holy Island). The Vikings attacked the monastery here in 793 CE.

SWORD NAMES

Swords were valuable and were given names, such as Leggbítr (Leg-biter) and Fótbítr (Foot-biter).

Warriors and Weapons

The main Viking weapon was the sword. It had a long iron blade and was used to chop at an enemy, not to stab with the point. Other weapons included spears with iron tips, bows and arrows, and heavy axes. A few warriors wore chain-mail armor made from tiny iron rings linked together. Warriors who could not afford chain mail wore leather jerkins (fitted jackets). Some wore iron helmets, but most made do with leather caps. Warriors carried round shields made from wood and leather.

 An iron helmet with bronze decoration from Sweden. It has a guard to protect the wearer's nose.

What Does it Tell Us?

This is the carving of a Viking "beserker" warrior. It shows the warrior biting on his shield. The bravest Viking warriors were called "beserkers." Before battle, they worked themselves into a rage—shouting and biting the edges of their shields. Our English expression "to go beserk" comes from the name of these fighters.

Families and Children

Family life was important to the Vikings. They helped family members with work, nursed one another in times of illness, and supported those who were too old or too sick to look after themselves.

Marriage

Viking men and women did not live as long as people do today—so Vikings married when they were teenagers. A marriage brought two families together. The groom (man) paid a sum of money for the bride (woman). This was known as the bride price. In return, the bride's father promised to hand over a dowry. This was a gift of money, goods, or property.

What Does it Tell Us?

At the center of every Viking longhouse was a hearth. This tells us that the hearth was very important to Viking family life. The hearth was an area of the house that contained a fire. It kept the house warm and food was cooked over it. At night, bedding was spread on the floor around the fire. Everyone in the family slept on the bedding around the fire, huddled close together to keep warm.

A Quick Wedding!

The groom and the bride's father shook hands, and the deal was done. The bride wasn't involved at all—she couldn't even choose her husband. On the wedding day, a feast was held at the bride's house, after which the couple began their new lives together.

Children

There were no schools for Viking children. Instead, they were expected to help their parents around the home, in the workshop, or on the farm.

Mothers taught their daughters how to **spin**, **weave**, and make clothes. Fathers taught their sons how to grow crops, look after animals, and make everyday things. Boys were taught how to make and use weapons also, and shown how to sail.

This is a replica of a Viking longhouse. Viking families lived inside houses such as this one. A hearth is at the center of the building and long benches to sit on are at the sides.

FAMILY FIGHTS

Families sometimes argued and this meant that a feud (long argument between families) began. They could last for years, and could be very violent with people being killed.

Gods and Religion

Most Vikings were **pagans**. Pagans had many different gods and goddesses, which they believed controlled the world.

Viking Religion

The Vikings thought their gods all lived in a place called Asgard. There were halls in Asgard, and one of them, called Valhalla, was the Viking version of heaven. The souls of dead warriors went to Valhalla, where they enjoyed lots of feasting and fighting in an **afterlife**.

Religious Feasts

There were no leaders of religion in Viking times. Instead, the king or important chieftains announced when religious feasts and festivals would happen. A feast was a time to give gifts to the gods. Animals and even humans were **sacrificed**, and in return for these gifts, Vikings hoped the gods would look after them.

 This church in Borgund, Norway, was built in the late 1100s from short, upright wooden posts called staves. It gives us a good idea of how a Christian Viking church looked.

The Main Gods

Balder	God of the sun and daylight
Frey	God of fertility
Freya	Goddess of fertility
Frigg	Goddess of women, the wife of Odin
Heimdall	Guardian of the bridge that joined earth to Asgard, the gods' home
Hel	God of the dead
Hermod	God of good deeds
Hoder	God of the night
Loki	God of trouble
Odin	King of the gods and god of knowledge and war
Thor	God of the sky, thunder, and strength
Tyr	God of war

A silver crucifix with an image of Jesus Christ. It would have been worn by a Christian Viking.

Christianity

The Vikings were some of the last people in Europe to become Christians. Between 1000 CE and 1100 CE, they abandoned their old gods and accepted the Christian god. This brought changes to the Viking way of life. Sacrifices stopped, and raids against fellow Christians in other parts of Europe ended.

THOR'S DAY

The English day of the week Thursday is named after the Viking god Thor (Thor's day).

What Does it Tell Us?

According to a Viking **myth**, Thor carried a mighty hammer called Mjöllnir. When he threw it, it always struck its target, then flew back into his hand. Viking craftworkers made lucky charms in the shape of Thor's hammer, such as this one (left). People wore the charms, believing that Thor's hammer would bring them good luck and protect them from harm.

21

Writing and Sagas

Some Vikings could read and write. They used letters called runes, which they believed had been discovered by Odin, king of the gods.

The Viking Alphabet

The Viking alphabet is known as the futhark. There were 24 runes in the first Viking alphabet, but later alphabets used just 16. All runes were made from short, straight lines. This made them easy to carve or scratch onto hard surfaces, such as wood and stone. Vikings carved runes wherever they went on their travels. Examples of rune carving have been found all over the Viking world, from Ireland to Turkey. Eventually, the Vikings began to use the Latin alphabet of 26 letters—the same one we use today.

What Does it Tell Us?

Rune stones were large stones put up to honor a dead person. The runes carved on them tell us about individual Vikings, their families, and what they had done when they were alive.

VIKING POETRY

Skalds were Viking poets. They used made-up words called kennings to describe things. For example, instead of saying "longship," they might say "horse of the sea" or "surf-dragon."

 This rune stone was found in Sweden. The markings on it say that it was put up by Helgulfr, in memory of his brother-in-law, Thorfastr.

Sagas

The Vikings told stories called **sagas**. They were long stories about the Viking gods, heroes, monsters, kings, and history. At first, all Viking sagas were spoken stories, passed on by word of mouth. Then, in the 1200s CE, they were written down for the first time. This is how Viking sagas have come down to us. If they had not been written down, the sagas would have disappeared without a trace, and we would know nothing about them.

This is part of a cross from the Isle of Man. It shows a scene from a Viking story about the god Odin being attacked by a wolf (his leg is in the wolf's mouth). Odin is stabbing at the wolf with his spear.

Sports and Games

The Vikings found many ways to entertain themselves. They enjoyed playing games and sports as well as music and singing. At night, they gathered around fires to listen to sagas and poems.

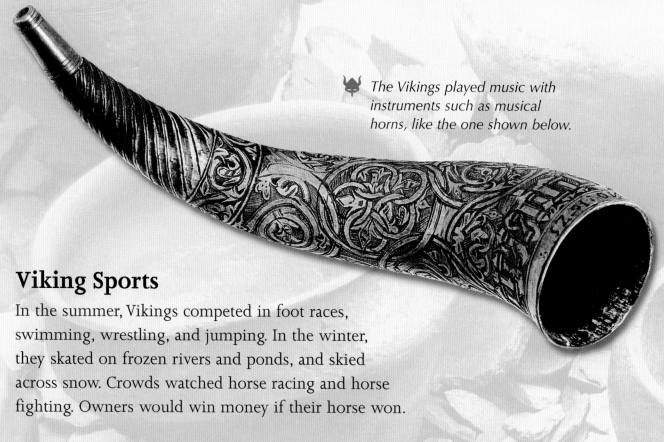

The Vikings played music with instruments such as musical horns, like the one shown below.

Viking Sports

In the summer, Vikings competed in foot races, swimming, wrestling, and jumping. In the winter, they skated on frozen rivers and ponds, and skied across snow. Crowds watched horse racing and horse fighting. Owners would win money if their horse won.

For some games, such as throwing rocks, competitors had to be fit and strong. Warriors took part in archery contests, shooting arrows into the center of a target. They also had sword fights. Both sports were good training for real fights and battles.

HEAVY SWIMMING

It is said that in some Viking swimming competitions, the competitors wore their heavy armor to make it more difficult.

Viking Games

Board games played with counters and dice were very popular. The best known board game was hnefatafl ("king's table"), which was for two players. The winner was the first person to capture their opponent's king. It was a game that needed clever thinking—just like chess. Chess became a popular game toward the end of the Viking Age. It may have been learned by Vikings who had traveled to the east.

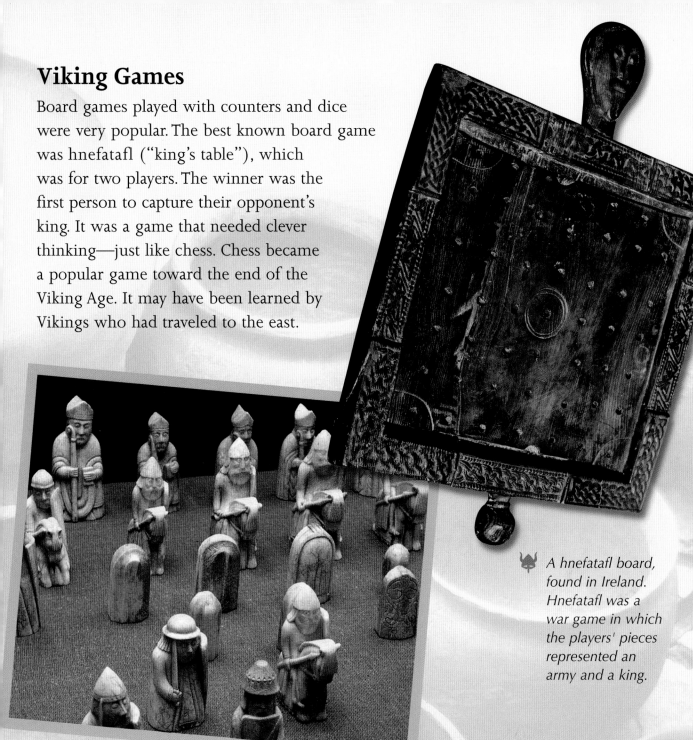

A hnefatafl board, found in Ireland. Hnefatafl was a war game in which the players' pieces represented an army and a king.

What Does it Tell Us?

This collection of Viking chess pieces was found on the Isle of Lewis, Scotland, in 1831. They had been carved in Norway from walrus ivory and whales' teeth. It shows us that some Vikings enjoyed playing chess.

Quiz

1. **When was the Viking Age?**
    a. 600 CE to 900 CE
    b. 800 CE to 1100 CE
    c. 1200 CE to 1500 CE

2. **Who lived inside a longhouse?**
    a. People only
    b. Farm animals only
    c. People and farm animals

3. **How many meals a day did Vikings have?**
    a. 1
    b. 2
    c. 3

4. **Which country did silk come from?**
    a. China
    b. Japan
    c. Russia

5. **Where was Vinland?**
    a. Canada
    b. Greenland
    c. Iceland

6. What were the bravest Viking warriors called?
a. Raiders
b. Skirmishers
c. Berserkers

7. What was a dowry?
a. A celebration meal
b. A type of coat
c. A gift of money, goods, or property

8. Who was king of the Viking gods?
a. Odin
b. Thor
c. Frey

9. What were individual Viking letters called?
a. Skalds
b. Runes
c. Futhark

10. The game of hnefatafl ("king's table") was played by how many players?
a. 2
b. 4
c. 6

ANSWERS

6. c.
7. c.   1. b.
8. a.   2. c.
9. b.   3. b.
10. a.   4. a.
               5. a.

Timeline

793 CE The first Viking raid in history, against a monastery on Lindisfarne, England.

c. 825 CE The first Viking coins are minted.

834–837 CE Viking raids against towns in Germany, along the Rhine River.

c. 800 CE A Viking longship is buried under a mound at Oseberg, Norway.

839 CE Vikings travel to Russia.

841 CE Viking settlers establish a base at Dublin, Ireland.

845 CE Vikings attack Paris, France, and Hamburg, Germany.

860 CE Vikings attack Constantinople (Istanbul), Turkey.

c. 860 CE Vikings explore the coast of Iceland.

862 CE Viking settlers establish a base at Novgorod, Russia.

865 CE An army of Vikings from Denmark invades England.

866 CE Vikings capture York, and it becomes their main town in England.

c. 870s CE Vikings begin to settle in Iceland.

876–879 CE Vikings begin to settle in eastern England.

886 CE England is divided in half—the north belongs to the Vikings, the south to the English.

902 CE The Vikings are thrown out of Dublin, Ireland.

c. 905 CE A Viking longship is buried under a mound at Gokstad, Norway.

912 CE Vikings begin to settle in northern France.

c. 965 CE Viking trade with the Middle East starts to slow down.

c. 985 CE Vikings begin to settle on Greenland, led by Erik the Red.

991 CE The Vikings force the English to pay ransom money to stop attacks on England.

995 CE Olaf Tryggvason becomes king of Norway and sets about converting the Vikings to Christianity.

c. 1000 CE Leif Ericsson, son of Erik the Red, explores the east coast of North America.

c. 1010 CE Viking explorer Thorfinn Karlsefni attempts to build a settlement in North America.

c. 1015 CE Vikings abandon their settlement in North America.

1066 CE A Viking army is defeated in England, at the Battle of Stamford Bridge.

1100 CE The Viking Age ends.

Glossary

abbot The head monk in a monastery, who is in charge of other monks.

afterlife A life believed to go on in a new place, after death in this world.

amber The fossilized resin from ancient trees, which is used to make jewelry.

bronze A yellowish metal mixed from copper and tin.

conquer To win people and land by using violence.

fjord A deep trench of water that runs inland from the sea.

glacier A mass of ice that moves slowly along a valley.

goods Things that are bought and sold.

ivory A tough, white material that makes up an elephant's tusks.

jet A black-colored precious stone.

mead An alcoholic drink made from honey and water.

monastery The building where monks live.

myth A well-known story that has been told for generations.

pagan A person who is not a Christian.

ransom Money paid to free a prisoner.

sacrifice Something done or given to make something happen, or please a god.

saga A long and detailed story or poem of Viking adventures.

settle To move into somewhere new and set up home.

slave A person who is someone else's property.

spin To twist bits of cotton or wool into thread.

stall A table outside that holds goods to be sold.

trader Someone who buys and sells goods.

tunic A piece of clothing a little like a dress, with a hole for the head and arms.

turf A layer of grass with roots and soil.

warrior A man who fights for his country, people, or money.

wattle and daub Interwoven twigs and poles covered with a thick layer of clay, straw, and manure.

weave To make fabric by crossing over strips of thread.

yeast A living substance that makes bread rise.

Further Information

Books

Everyday Life in Viking Times
by Hazel Mary Martell
(Sea to Sea Publications, 2005)

How People Lived in Viking Times
by Colin Hynson
(PowerKids Press, 2008)

The Vikings
by Virginia Schomp
(Children's Press, 2005)

Web Sites

Due to the changing nature of Internet links, PowerKids Press has developed an online list of Web sites related to the subject of this book. This site is updated regularly. Please use this link to access this list: http://www.powerkidslinks.com/dig/vikings

Index